Words from This Life

Jason Crowley

Fulton Books
Meadville, PA

Published by Fulton Books 2024

ISBN 979-8-89221-759-0 (paperback)
ISBN 979-8-89221-760-6 (digital)

Printed in the United States of America

CONTENTS

ACKNOWLEDGEMENT

For Kathy. Thank you for being beside me.

My soul was reassigned in 1965.

Things come into my mind and get sucked out,
Like leaves in a wind tunnel.

INSIDE OUT

All my other lives overwhelm me,
With details or none.
The burden is there,
From every one.
The thought of my feelings making it to words,
Exhausts and drains me.
I think I am a bully to myself.
There are more than just me inside,
And we don't like each other much.
Rarely do we pass up the chance
To make ourselves feel,
Undeserving of even our own acceptance.
My smile is a bandage,
My laughter a salve.
But neither stops the infection or pain.
Fear, and the memory of fear,
Seep through the cracks inside.
And so I hide,
As I tear myself down,
From the inside out.

THE EDGE OF NOWHERE

I've been there.
Please hear me.
You're standing alone on the edge of nowhere.
You feel like there is nothing in front of you,
Nothing to move you along to just one more day.
There are no more smiles,
No laughs left inside,
Nothing left but to die.
You are not alone.
Even when you're standing on the edge of nowhere,
You are not alone.
There are others,
And we are here.
I know you feel it can't be true,
But you have it inside you to keep going.
You are not alone.
There are others,
We are here.
Take a step away from the edge,
You are strong,
You can go on.
I've been there.
You're standing alone on the edge of nowhere.

You feel you don't have the energy to stay.
Stay anyway.
Someone needs you.
There are still smiles.
There are still laughs.
There is still love.
I know you feel it can't be true,
But you have it inside you to keep going.
You are not alone.
There are others.
We are here.
There is still hope.
There are others,
And we are still here.
Be here with us.

REALITY FADES

I find myself moving too fast from
Moment to moment.
In the moments in between, in the
Moments we miss, reality fades.
From the time we emerge from our dreams each day,
And sometimes before,
Our thoughts are many steps away into the day.
They scurry away from us into
The chaos of expectation.
I've got to remember not to forget,
All the things that need doing.
Another reminder fills my brain, but
There's no more room there.
Don't we know there is so much to do?
And before we realize the day is through.
I don't want to miss the moments;
They are all that we have.
In the end, we'll be wishing for
Just one more moment.
Just one more moment watching your smile.
Just one more moment in the warmth of your hug.
Just one more moment lost in your eyes.

Just one more moment holding your hand,
While we feel the wind on our faces,
While we breathe in the air,
While we watch the blue sky, the sunset, the clouds.
I'll try to find a way to settle my mind.
A way to place that picture of my
Last moment with you,
Forever in my mind.
So that I will grasp every moment,
And all the in-between moments,
And never again let my reality fade.

TELL ME A STORY

Let fly the mind,
Show me what's inside.
Tell me a story, take me away,
Get me through another day.
Dreams full of dreams and wondrous things,
Riding emotions from laughter to screams.
Into the darkness safe from the light,
Chasing my madness to conquer my fright.
Let fly the world,
Show me what's inside.
Build me new moments to take me away,
Help me through another day.
Memories with daydreams build wondrous things,
Growing emotions suspend disbelief.
Running through shadows mocking what scares,
I push myself deeper weaving nightmares.
Let fly your thoughts,
Show me what you've got.
Tell me a story, take me away,
Drag me through another bad day.
Regrets under smiles are powerful things,
Just under the laughter a mournful scream.

6

Running from yesterdays, keep them at bay,
Falling further from me, away far away.
Let fly the pain,
Show me how I go on.
Tell me a story, make me strong.
Please help me make it through one more day.
Tell me a story.
Just tell me a story.

DON'T DIE QUIET

Fade in, fade out.
Speak up before your lights go out.
Paint your world and words.
Let yourself be heard.
We only walk this life for a little while,
Don't die quiet.
The play goes on and on, what's your line?
Don't die quiet.
What they think, forget it.
Be who you are, stand up for it.
What's your identity?
This is infinity.
We only walk this life for a little while,
Don't die quiet.
The play goes on and on, what's your line?
Don't die quiet.

I AM AWARE

The gremlins of my past,
Are in the rearview mirror.
To those who gave them voice,
You have no place here.
Every day's a gift.
In your dark I shine.
I start and end each day now with a smile.
I am aware.
I am aware.
Breathe deep, breathe through.
I no longer do what you want me to,
Because I'm aware of you.
Once upon a time,
You stalked the corners of my mind.
But you're tamed now,
No more wasting my time.
Every day's a gift.
All that weight is lifted.
I spend my day with friendly voices,
And I listen.
I am aware.
I am aware.
Breathe deep, breathe through.

I no longer do what you want me to,
Because I'm aware of you.
I'm crystal clear,
My heart is here,
You're a nowhere man.
My life is mine,
You're old storylines,
A failing plan.
And every day's a gift,
All that weight is lifted.
I spend my day with friendly voices.

THE EXCAVATION OF ME

It is widely felt, at least I've heard it said,
That your soul leaves your body
In the moment of death.
That is not how it was with me,
As the doctors worked, and I struggled to breathe.
I remember the moment, I remember the scene,
It was well before my heart stopped,
When my essence, my soul if you
Like, let go and drifted free.
It was a slow thing, I felt that reality grow thin,
The pain began fading, with brief shocks of dismay.
And as I wafted away from who I had been,
The dismay followed the pain and was finally away.
I floated so slightly up to above,
Where I watched myself dying
Despite efforts and love.
My last breath came with similar
Fanfare to my first years before.
Those in attendance shook their
Heads and walked out the door.
With the gloves removed, sheets pulled,
And the lights turned down,
I drifted away gently, the only soul around.

I could not say how much time then passed,
Time now being a different thing for me,
But the light seemed to change around me at last,
And I was suddenly hovering in the
Desert sun on the edge of a sea.
It was evidently ungodly hot, not that I could feel,
But those below were sweating
And digging with zeal.
There was some excitement when
Another artifact was found,
Bring it to me, a woman said, her
Voice a comforting sound.
She brushed it off and placed it next
To the others in a woodbin.
They were pieces of me, or at least
The me I had just been.
We're down to the year 2000, someone
Said, studying the earth.
Not a great year I recall, thirty-five from my birth.
I continued to drift above watching their progress,
As they made their way down through my life.
You may think that I suffered feeling distress,
Watching pieces of who I had been
Brought into the sunlight.
But there was no remorse, no regret, no sense of loss,
When the soul passes over, the emotions can't cross.

I suppose it must be that way, or
We'd all go mad with grief,
When we're reassigned, for another try.
It makes me wonder if those we
Encounter wandering the streets,
Who suffer from such madness and
Pain, we watch them cry,
Are souls who had their emotions slip
Through when they crossed.
But let's not get lost in such deep
And depressing thoughts,
Back to the story of the excavation of me.
They were working hard in the dirt,
Down and down they'd go,
Find my first love, I think,
Find what became of my hope.
Hope could be a thing which never is found,
Before, while, or after you're around.
Although I believe my hope was here
And gone and back again,
As I wandered through the man I'd been.
Then they pulled from the site,
Cleaned and cataloged,
My first kiss, and I felt the where and the when.
The sweetest of moments, oh, so sweet Lynn.
That one got through; a feeling crossed over.

A tinge of sadness to ponder.
Then I looked at the pieces of me lying in the sun,
And I saw it there bright and fresh, Kathy, the one.
She was my love and my life and now I was gone.
The pain and loss that hit me could
Not be stopped by any barrier,
No natural or supernatural wall
Could keep that pain from me.
I willed myself away, not having it
In me to suffer such grief.
But just then they found the first time I sang.
Then they found the first song I wrote.
The first story, first poem,
First lyric, the first painting,
And a tinge of joy leaked through.
If I'd still had a mouth, I may have smiled.
If I'd still had a heart, I may have felt it warm.
Then it was gone, and I was back to floating empty.
With nowhere to go and nothing to feel.
I thought, *Tell me when you make it back to sixty-five*,
I'm told I arrived in early January late at night.
I wonder if in that moment,
The pain and memories came rushing back,
And that scream and cry, when
They smacked my ass,
Was more about remembering what I'd lost,

In my last life, if only for a moment.
I guess, if I am to have another chance,
If I am to have another shot,
I'll find out soon enough.
A breeze kicked up and I drifted away.
I turned from the deconstruction of
Who I had been before,
And wondered what was now in store.
Who will I be?
Will I remember the things that hurt?
Will I remember the joy?
Will I remember things that I learned?
What me awaits me?
Will I find it in me,
To be a better person this time around?

ECHOES AND WHISPERS

The things I've done are my echo.
They are the things that make me proud.
But for every echo, there is a whisper.
That's me inside, tearing myself down.
We all want to scream from the mountain,
See me! Look at what I did!
But hiding inside, shaking with fear,
Is that forever scared little kid.
No matter what I've been able to achieve,
It never seems to be enough,
To settle that shaking,
Or calm that fear.
Sometimes the scared little child,
Becomes a nightmare gremlin,
Laughing, and tearing apart,
The things that make me smile.
I'll keep trying,
To comfort the shaking child.
I'll keep trying,
To shine a light on the darkness of that gremlin.

Until one is warm and safe,
And the other is beaten and gone.
Until then, I'll keep screaming from the mountain,
Because that's where our echoes belong.

END OF IT ALL

It's been a long and winding road,
Full of tears and smiles.
From sunsets to starry, starry nights,
Cool winds and autumn skies.
On we go,
Down the road.
So many years behind me,
How many more to go?
Thank you for being beside me.
See how the time has faded,
Where does it go?
Thank you for being beside me,
At the end of it all.
A little child he's up on a hill.
Can you feel him?
He's in there still.
No one's getting to him this time.
The kid's alright and I'm just fine.
On we go,
Down the road.
So many years behind me,
How many more to go?
Thank you for being beside me.

See how the time has faded,
Where does it go?
Thank you for being beside me,
At the end of it all.
There are beer stains on my lyrics,
And stories in my mind.
I dip a pen and paintbrush in my soul,
Leave pieces of myself behind.

HARD SMILE

So many miles,
On an unforgiving road.
Never giving up,
I've got to carry the load.
I've got a road map for my soul,
I've got my heart in tow.
Taking it day by day,
It's the only way to go.
Running from everything I wanted for me.
Running into the man I used to be.
Running from you, are you running from me?
Running into the man I used to be.
It's a hard smile.
Life keeps pushing me away.
It's a hard smile.
Still I'm smiling anyway.
Grinding and grinding,
Time on top of time.
Take another piece of me,
And toss it to the side.
Dream after dream,
And all that I love,
Everything I've done,

It's never quite enough.
Just a little longer,
Rest is overrated.
You know you must be perfect,
Or else you will be hated.
Pushing you, I'm pushing you,
I've got to be just right.
Hurry up now,
You're wasting light.
Running from everything I wanted for me.
Running into the man I used to be.
Running from you, are you running from me?
Running into the man I used to be.
It's a hard smile.
Life keeps pushing me away.
It's a hard smile.
Still I'm smiling anyway.

FEAR

Forty days and forty nights.
When is this storm going to blow out of sight?
The bars are open, and the beer is cold.
You've got to stay strong because it's not over.
Hello again,
It's been too long.
I'm back again,
And you thought I was gone.
But I was here,
Hiding in the dark.
In the shadows,
Waiting to tear you apart.
Fear.
Forty days and forty nights.
Tears or rain, it's all the same.
Your eyes are open, but your mind is numb.
You've got to stay strong because here I come.
Hello again,
It's been too long.
I'm back again,
And you thought I was gone.
But I was here,
Hiding in the dark.

In the shadows,
Waiting to tear you apart.
Fear.
Wander in the desert, wonder your mind.
Trying to decide if I'm still alive.
The clouds tear open and hope rains down.
You've got to stay strong because I'm still around.
Hello again,
It's been too long.
I'm back again,
And you thought I was gone.
But I was here,
Hiding in the dark.
In the shadows,
Waiting to tear you apart.
Fear.

HOPE IN THE WIND

From time to time, it happens still,
I close my eyes and drift away to dream.
Then suddenly, I'm floating, I'm flying.
I'm above, watching the world below me.
I fill my lungs, and it lifts me higher.
I'm above the world.
I'm taken by the wind.
I tuck, then swoop, I dive,
The power surge,
The sudden urge,
To do what thou wilt.
As Aleister felt.
But it's just a dream.
It's just a dream.
From time to time, it happens still,
I open my eyes and breathe in the wonderful air.
I feel the wind all around me and I'm alive.
I look around me and I'm struck
With the wonder of the world.
I'm struck with the wonder of life,
And how lucky I am.
I close my eyes and my heart fills with hope.
Hope, the most elusive of things.

Hope, the thing of dreams.
Hope, the thing that drives you mad,
When you have it and then it's gone.
Hope, the thing that drives you mad,
When you look and look but cannot find it.
Where does it go…hope?
It's like a magic trick that only
Works some of the time.
It's a luxury and a necessity all at once.
If I could just fly like I can in my dreams,
Then maybe I could chase hope around the sky,
And force it down to the ground
Where we all need it.
That would be a wonderful dream indeed,
But it's just a dream.
It's just a dream.
Still, I can hope.

CASUALTY OF TIME

(With contributions from Vincent Simon)

I'm leaking energy,
And I don't remember me.
Too many yesterdays,
And everything fades away.
I keep looking to the sky,
To see where the sun might shine.
Tossed away like I was never there.
There I was and here I am.
I can't find myself again.
I keep looking to the sky,
To see where the sun might shine.
Hello from the end of the rainbow.
I'm just down here looking for my soul.
I'm a casualty of time,
Life has passed me by.
If you can spare it, I could use some hope.
Save your bullshit bedtime stories,
I'll take the real world, please.
Don't mind the words I say,
It's just laughter wrapped around pain.
I must have been left on your doorstep.

Do you even care who I am?
My whole life's been one big gut check.
Finding peace wherever I can.
I keep looking to the sky,
To see where the sun might shine.
Hello from the end of the rainbow.
I'm just down here looking for my soul.
I'm a casualty of time,
Life has passed me by.
If you can spare it,
I could use some hope.
Hello from the end of the rainbow.
I'm just down here looking for my soul.
I'm a casualty of time,
Life has passed me by.
If you can spare it, I could use some hope.
Save your bullshit bedtime stories,
I'll take the real world, please.
Don't mind.
Don't mind.
Don't mind.
Don't mind.

SOMEWHERE BETWEEN DREAMS

Somewhere in the twilight between dreams,
Floating softly through the air,
We tumble numbly into memories,
We are circles turning circles 'round the square.
I remember little moments with fading smiles,
And wishing hard for things beyond me.
I remember sudden movements breaking silence,
And wishing away the things I would see.
Times of warmth and the brightest sunshine,
Laughter all around; surround me, friends.
Times I look back now and seek to find,
And wish those days to never end.
Moments on moments build the life,
Wrapped up in the memory of days.
Smiles mixed with tears fill the mind.
Forever together in the tale.
Share, no matter how hard the journey.
Believe, no matter how dark the sky.
Persevere, no matter the difficulty.
Shine your light until the clouds pass by.

Somewhere in the twilight between dreams,
Floating softly through the air,
We tumble numbly into memories,
We are circles turning circles 'round the square.

Too much bouncing around.
My mind just won't keep still.
Empty pages abound.
Another Jay brain spill.
Oh, I've got something to say.
And you don't have to listen.
Feel free to walk away.
Sit down, shut up.
That's never been my thing.
It's the only way I know.
It's my human being.
And I don't give a damn,
If you don't understand.
I don't care if you don't see.
That's never mattered to me.
Sometimes you think you're done,
When the river doesn't run.
Just get out of your own way,
And let it come.
I've got something to say.
And you don't have to listen.
Feel free to walk away.

PIECES OF ME

You know there used to be a time,
When I was lost in my own mind.
But those days are all long gone.
I've moved on and on and on.
A simple selfish relief,
Taking care of me.
I don't want to be you.
I found my way back home.
I'm not going to feed you,
Any more pieces of me.
And I won't believe you.
I found my way back home.
I'm not going to feed you.
You know I put myself through hell,
The way that I would always dwell.
I don't blame anyone but me.
We're always where we choose to be.
Don't put up with fear and doubt.
You've got to take that garbage out.
It's just a sorry self-attack,
And I won't be dragged back.
I don't want to be you.
I found my way back home.

I'm not going to feed you,
Any more pieces of me.
And I won't believe you.
I found my way back home.
I'm not going to feed you.
No more.

SPIRITS AND LIFELINES

I stand on the shoulders of the voices in my mind.
I stand on the shoulders of the lives I've left behind.
In my dreams, they weave the thoughts I capture.
Over and over runs the film of my life.
Spirits and lifelines,
Welcome to my time.
There's no one left behind.
Spirits and lifelines.
I see the faces in the clouds look down and scream.
If I don't tell their stories, they'll come back for me.
There's lightning in the sky, and I don't know why.
Pieces of the past keep coming back to me.
Spirits and lifelines,
Welcome to my time.
There's no one left behind.
Spirits and lifelines.
It's midnight all the time, and
nothing seems to soothe.
I've got too much to lose by feeling the truth.
I hear the tune, I toast the moon, it's there for me.
I write the words as they're heard from deep in me.

Spirits and lifelines,
Welcome to my time.
There's no one left behind.
Spirits and lifelines.

GYPSY ME

I've been on the run so long.
I don't know where I'm going.
Some may say I'm lost,
But I am wandering.
I'd find my way back home,
But I don't have one.
I hopped a ride,
On my train of thought.
I had no ticket,
So I got tossed off.
I lost myself,
Somewhere down the line.
I found myself,
In the nick of time.
Sometimes I feel like I'm a gypsy.
I've got nowhere to go,
But I don't care.
Memories eat at me like a vulture.
The best part of me,
Torn from the bone.
My shiny reality,
It all went wrong.

Erase myself,
Replace me with a song.
Sometimes I feel like I'm a gypsy.
I've got nowhere to go,
But I don't care.

Stupid expectations.
Right brain standing still.
Don't throw away your every day.
Educate yourself.
The sun is shining inside.
Don't let yourself forget.
Music is your lifeline.
You know you aren't done yet.
So while you're killing time,
You're only wasting light.
There's still too much to say.
Don't let it waste away.
Look around, this is the old days.
Live it now before it's gone.
Look around, this is the old days.
It's yesterday before too long.
Silly imitations.
Passing far too long.
Don't throw away your every day.
Throw it into song.
Don't be in the wrong place,
Because this is the right time.

Grab hold of yourself.
Step out of line.
Righteous variations.
The powerful play goes on.
Don't throw away your every day.
Oh me, oh life.
We're here and who knows why?
Leave your mark upon it,
Because time is flying by.
Look around, this is the old days.
Live it now before it's gone.
Look around, this is the old days.
It's yesterday before too long.

FIND ME

(With contributions from Dan Lesko)

Can you show me the way,
Or maybe just stay awhile?
Because I was hoping to play,
But I would settle for a smile.
I feel like hiding from the day.
Could I hide inside with you awhile?
We'll bolt the door and say, go away.
Then we'll run and we will hide.
Can you find me?
Look between the lines and to the edge.
Would you like me,
To lose myself in space and time?
Can you find me?
Look between the lines and to the edge.
Would you like me,
To lose myself in space and time?
Can you feel me today?
The sun is up, but I can't see.
I feel I'm slipping away.
Losing touch with reality.

But it doesn't matter anyway,
Because I'm getting sick of this ride.
I've said all there is to say.
So, I'll see you on the other side.
Can you show me the way,
Or maybe just stay awhile?
Because I was hoping to play,
But I would settle for a smile.
I feel like hiding from the day.
Could I hide inside with you awhile?
We'll bolt the door and say, go away.
Then we'll run and we will hide.

DAY'S FIRST LIGHT

The sun comes up,
On the deep blue horizon.
Shafts of light,
Fall like shards of broken glass.
Off in the distant night,
Wails a child in constant pain.
Bringing back the dark of night,
To appearance of day's first light.
Day's first light.
The moon dies slowly,
Into the shadow of the hills.
Fears of night,
Fall beyond the wall inside.
They burrow deep,
Beneath the fatty cells and brain waves.
Activity acts as the building stone,
To keep them away.
Day's first light.
In an instant situation,
Comes the wrecking ball.
It swings in silence,
Crushing stones inside the child's mind.

41

Fear, and the memory of fear,
Crash through the crack inside.
Furiously thinking, time to time.
You try to keep them all away.
Day's first light.
Keep them all away.
Stay away.

Before My Eyes

Coming soon is a different page.
And so, I watch myself wasting away.
Like a movie from the balcony.
Down in front, it's so hard to see.
I see you vanishing before my eyes.
I can feel you wasting away.
It doesn't matter how hard I try.
I can see you vanishing before my eyes.
The lights go out, the room is black.
A stream of light shoots from above me.
Splitting the darkness like an angel.
Like an angry angel.
It hits the wall to give me an eyeful.
I can see you vanishing before my eyes.
I can feel you slipping away.
It just doesn't matter how hard I try.
I see you vanishing before my eyes.
The beginning was quite slow.
I seemed to be having trouble communicating.
But once I grasped the English language,
I found my costars participating.
I see you vanishing before my eyes.
I can feel you slipping away.

It just doesn't matter how hard I try.
I can see you vanishing before my eyes.
Frame to frame, I cover my face.
Remembering all my stupid mistakes.
No matter, I thought, I live and learn.
I'll try to fix it on my next turn.
I see you vanishing before my eyes.
I can feel you wasting away.
It just doesn't matter how hard I try.
I see you vanishing before my eyes.

TRIBE

To belong,
To be a part of something,
Is to be inside strong.
Being part of the tribe and not just being.
To share,
To let others in,
Is to be a part of something,
More than just who you've been.
To fear,
Yet still embrace the opening of you,
Is to grow,
Until your inside strong shines through.
To accept,
To accept who you are,
Is to conquer your fear,
And find together hidden in the apart.
To belong,
To be a part of something,
Is to be inside strong.
Being part of the tribe and not just being.

I flinch.
My breath escapes.
The panic takes me,
And I duck inside.
I hide away,
Until the danger is gone.
Closing my eyes,
I make myself small,
So it cannot get me.
I slip away into another place,
Until the danger is gone.
If I stay here, in the dark,
Maybe it will go away.
Maybe soon, it will be safe.
Maybe soon, I can be safe.
If I keep my eyes closed,
If I stay in here,
If I build another world,
Maybe it will go away.
If I make the sun shine here,
If I make some friends here,
If I spend my day here,
Maybe everything will be okay.

Maybe if I find someone to save here,
Maybe if I find a hero who saves the day,
Maybe, just maybe,
It will go away.
If I listen close,
Maybe I can hear the storm still,
Out there from where I escaped.
Until I hear the silence,
I'll stay here where I'm safe.

How It Used to Be

The child inside can stop the world to play with me.
He's found the ancient rhyme of memory.
Finding bits and pieces of you and me.
He's a collector, building worlds of fantasy.
Bringing back the pictures of yesterday.
Wondering why it all went away.
Finding ourselves and coming home,
To how it used to be.
But hate is still in place behind the dream.
An ever-present state of reality.
He's looking for a trapdoor to lose the lies,
Somewhere safely back in time.
I started thinking about what I was thinking about.
Remember what it was when it was then?
Staring through the window to another place.
Seeing miles away through time and space.
Bringing back the pictures of yesterday.
Wondering why it all went away.
Finding ourselves and coming home,
To how it used to be.

So superior,
Wish I could be you.
Such a mask you wear,
If only it were true.
Empty words,
It's not who you are.
How many dents,
In your soul so far?
Another inferior,
You think to yourself.
Secure in the knowledge,
He's going to hell.
To you,
They're all just wasted spaces.
You claim the high ground,
From both your faces.
Push that truth away.
Skip high and mighty,
Through another day.
It's too bad,
You're not who you claim to be.
But all that matters is you feel alright.

49

At least you know,
You're better than me.
So you can sleep at night.
Please look the other way, you say.
That doesn't concern us.
As you fake your way through another day.
You're a Friday night Jesus.
Show everyone the picture perfect you.
But we know it isn't true.
You think you can deceive us.
You're just a Friday night Jesus.

I saw a boulder bouncing downhill,
Into a crowded house.
I felt a bullet inside my brain,
Planting mental grain.
I said to misty ghostly friends,
In the attic in my head,
Now it's harvest time again.
What have you got for me today?
What have you got for me,
This time around?
I saw crystal in the ball,
Melt away from you.
It was a vision in my mind,
At high noon yesterday.
Who would have thought,
I had a care about the life of you.
I guess it's reflective vindication,
For the time you went away.
What have you got for me today?
What have you got for me,
This time around?
It's like the storybook,
And all the pages in between.

It's only dreaming,
Still, you wake up with a scream.
And so, I'm writing,
Until my fingers ache from yesterday.
The story always ends the same,
With nothing left of me.
What have you got for me today?
What have you got for me,
This time around?

WELCOME TO THE CHANGE

Reality,
Contaminate this fairy tale.
The storyline's been lost,
But not forgotten.
Time,
Evaporate this wishing well.
Listen to all my coins hit bottom.
Visions of the past,
Keeping my heart tied down.
Cradling all my memories,
In my hand.
Let a little life seep in,
While it's flying by.
Let the healing begin,
While I cry.
We'd like to welcome you home, my friend.
Welcome to the change.
We'd like to welcome your dream's end.
Welcome to the change.
There are bits and pieces of dreams,
Breaking up on the reef,
And gasping for air.

Floating in a shambles,
Toward never-never land,
On the tide of time,
They'll get there when they can.

WAY BACK WHEN

(With contributions from Dan Lesko)

All my life it seems,
I'm staring down a dream.
Thinking of the other times,
And all my other lives.
So today, it wanders by,
And I sit and wonder why.
And I look but I can't find,
I can't find my peace of mind.
If I could only be there,
Just to do it all again.
Time keeps sliding,
To way back when.
Like echoes in the wind,
I'm feeling where I've been.
All the flashes of the past,
They keep on coming back.
And I'm hearing,
I'm hearing what you said.
And I know, I finally know,
It's all in my head.

If I could only be there,
Just to do it all again.
Time keeps sliding,
Slipping and sliding,
To way back when.
If I could only be there,
Just to do it all again.
Through time I'm sliding,
I'm sliding to way back when.

AN OLD MAN'S DREAM

Said the old man to the sunshine,
Once more around the outside.
Oh, we must get to the last one,
To be ready when the rains come.
How long now until we see you,
Come to sell us what we don't know?
In a bad dream comes the answer,
To the questions about the next show.
Lazy paint days on an old farm.
Hear the milkmen in the old barn.
Numbing buzzwords meaning nothing,
Creeping sweetly in a soft dream.
It's okay now, close your eyes.
Breathing deep, escape inside.
It doesn't matter what we don't know.
Fall away, world weight, it's time to go.

Float away,
To a shiny crystal play.
Do the dialogue,
As you move away.
All those pictures of yourself,
When you were young,
Cast shadows on you now,
And so, you run.
Now it's 2 a.m.,
And the night is getting long.
It's 2 a.m.,
And the water's getting warm.
Come fight for me,
If you feel like letting on,
That you still see me,
And what's going on is wrong.
Vast degrading rhymes,
Transcending time,
They catch you.
When your soul is set to fly,
They take away your heart and eyes,
Then stand by laughing as you slowly die.

Whispers first.
Is someone there?
I thought I heard the rocking chair.
A faint fragrance, an old man's pipe.
They gather, waiting, until the time is right.
Late at night by the fireplace.
They feel there's no more time to waste.
An instant later, my fingers fury.
Words on words without a worry.
I hear them here, loud and clear.
Waiting while I weep and cheer.
I like these things these voices say.
But wonder will they go away?
Is this my muse?
I start to sweat.
Or has my sanity up and left?
What's the difference, I stop the thought.
I'll simply write and worry not.

Once upon a time,
Said the man.
You're flying blind,
So take my hand.
We slipped past the bookcase,
To a spiraling stairway.
Down through the shadows,
The hourglass and sand.
Through layers of dust,
And buried mistakes.
Into the dark,
Saying "Catch me if you can."
A chance to dream the pain away.
No more screams, so dream away.
The past is gone, the voices say.
No more screams, so dream away.
It seems we're just in time,
Said the man.
Your heart is still alive,
Then we ran.
Into the attic,
We flew through time.

To dig up the innocence,
Of an innocent man.
With snapshots of happy,
We cleared out my mind.
Screaming to no one,
"Catch me if you can."
A chance to dream the pain away.
No more screams, so dream away.
The past is gone, the voices say.
No more screams, so dream away.
Once upon a time,
Said the man.
I had to save my life,
From my own hand.
I'd wished on the wrong stars,
And ran down the wrong path.
That led to another,
Much darker and poor.
I've come through much wiser,
Though still wish on stars.
But the child that's inside me,
Isn't buried anymore.

Second Chances

Don't you ever forget.
Don't let yourself die.
It's yet another clean slate,
Another try.
Just remember everything you've done.
Now come and meet me back at square one.
Reset, erase, rewind.
Now do it one more time.
What would you give to do it all again?
What would you give for second chances?
I know I've lived through bullshit now and then.
Still, I live for second chances.
I can feel this life is almost spent.
I sit around and wonder where it all went.
I feel the joy is fading,
I feel the fear.
It's falling all around me,
Year after year.
See my changing faces.
See all the same old places.
I'm waiting for another chance at life,
As I wander,
Back and forth through time.

Reset, erase, rewind.
Now do it one more time.
What would you give to do it all again?
What would you give for second chances?
I know I've lived through bullshit now and then.
Still, I live for second chances.

Indian summer,
I'm on the brink of another,
Mistake.
Blinded by sunshine,
Given my lifetime,
Twisting my faith.
Hopeless romantic,
Lost in a panic,
Changing how I dream.
Reliving the future,
Ready the sutures,
Here come the screams.
Headfirst.
Dive in the deep end.
Learning to swim again.
I'm holding my breath again.
I might as well dive in,
Headfirst.
Feel like I'm dreaming,
I'm losing my reason,
Bring on the strife.

Guided by nothing,
Searching for something,
With a little life.
Surrounded by sorrow,
What happens tomorrow,
Runs through my mind.
Forgetting the last time,
I'm living my lifetime,
I cover my eyes.
Probably screaming,
I have no more feeling,
In my heart.
Believing the morals,
Of fairy-tale stories,
I'm tired of this part.
Wishing on bright stars,
Suffering downfalls,
Keeps me up at night.
Traveling numb,
Through life without sun,
Keeps me out of sight.

WHEN YOU CAN'T SEE YOURSELF

The crystal cracked,
One lonely night,
And soon after,
The mirror followed.
I could no longer see myself,
When I stared there.
So I packed my things,
And went searching for another.
Sooner or later,
This will happen to you.
What you knew,
And who you are,
Will become unclear.
When that happens,
And the moment presents itself,
All you can do is look inside,
And start again.
Once in a while,
Someone may step in,
If your place in the world warrants.
But don't count on it.
Don't count on anything.

The only constant will be,
You are on your own.
I came to a road,
I seem to recall,
And thought about it long and hard.
Surely, I'd been there before.
Still searching,
I ignored myself and walked on.

BREATHE

Insightful riots rumble in dream sequence.
Shouts of silence whisper woes of vengeance.
Keeping calm provides the eye of triumph,
Bringing back the future's jesting judgment.
Look along the line of dead man's spirit,
To the day when waves and waves of cheer,
Wash upon the broken glass of yesterday,
Turning burning grains of sand to gems.
Dream away, we say,
But rarely do we.
Practice not the preached divine.
Instead, we choose to only breathe.
To improve,
We respectfully decline.
Breathe,
Blinks the eye.
Beat,
Thinks the heart.
Breathe,
Beats the heart song.
Breathe.

WON'T YOU COME OUT AND PLAY?

You've stepped inside yourself.
Have you bolted all the doors?
The curtains are drawn,
And the soundtrack is on.
So, you're playing pieces of the past.
I see you.
Won't you come out and play?
You wander down the path of yesterday,
Looking for the ones you missed.
An invisible wind changed your direction.
You never saw the life you left.
Won't you put the past away?
I feel you.
Won't you come out and play?
The days are full of loss of emotion.
Absorb it but don't bat an eye.
No one taught you self-contrition.
Don't let the inside run dry.

I just felt like writing this down.
It's the middle of the night,
And there's no one around.
Maybe come morning,
I'll have second thoughts.
But now it's only me,
And that's good enough.
There's a story,
Hiding in my head.
But life,
Gets in the way instead.
Alternating currents,
Bring it into view.
A piece of my puzzle,
Not just a tune.
Life's a field,
Where your heart can feed.
Do we get what we want,
Or just what we need?
The sooner you realize,
The later it feels.
Tomorrow is coming,
On yesterday's heels.

DAYS GONE BY

Why not take some time to reflect,
On the things we've seen.
Why not sit a while and think,
About when and where we've been.
I think a lot about yesterday.
How did it get so far away?
Once upon a midnight dream,
Starry skies and a soft sad breeze.
We sat and wondered to each other,
How we'd feel when we remembered.
Such a long and lonely time ago.
Trying hard to not let go.
Caught between the now and when.
Feeling both the begin and the end.
You can't bring back the days gone by.
Just try to smile and remember.
Just try to smile for forever.

DONE WITH THE ANGELS

That's it, I'm done.
This was the last time.
No more wasting light.
I'm done with the angels.
I wonder why I never noticed,
You're so much better than me.
I'm back and forth from hurt to anger,
Hoping for apathy.
How dare I ask for your time,
It's more important than mine.
There's no room on your pedestal,
I'll step down.
That's it, I'm done.
This was the last time.
No more wasting light.
I'm done with the angels.
Everything seems to insult you,
As if you're under attack.
No one lives up to your perfection.
Why can't you just relax?
How dare I ask for your time,
It's more important than mine.

There's no room on your pedestal,
We'll all step down.
What you're describing is life.
To live you find the time.
It's something we all do.
Why can't you?
That's it, I'm done,
This was the last time.
No more wasting light.
I'm done with the angels.

EXPECTATIONS

What are your expectations today?
Relief in some form, I would say.
Grazing cattle in the country sun,
Working very hard for no one.
Whatever it takes,
I really hate that phrase.
It seems to be the expected mental state.
Ghosts in the form of decision,
An invasion of my vision.
Someone once said that no one ever said…
Fill in the blank with your own cliché.
We've got centuries of quotation.
Have you heard the phrase…*out-of-date*?
I read today,
Of a town far away,
Buried in a landslide.
They found a survivor,
Only one.
He won't come out,
He's getting too much done.

Rise and smell the stop signs,
Is my surreal cliché.
If I put it on a T-shirt,
I'll make a lot of money,
Or so they say.

Working back to the rhyme.
I know it's not the way,
But who am I to say?
Search the words we're out to find.
A safer place to congregate.
Looking through the broken glass,
I reflect upon the bad days ahead of me.
I see a soft and sleepy scene,
Where I feel a distant scream,
But not my heartbeat.
And I decline to authorize,
The shipment of my soul to infinity.
I'll take the title, please,
Now that it's all over,
Because I've paid my fees.
I'd like my name engraved in stone,
On my shady country home,
Near a quiet little stream.
And I'll listen through the years,
To a steady stream of tears,
But in a peaceful dream.

FOOL IN THE MIRROR

Is this my real life?
Have I been dreaming?
Don't stay lost inside.
Don't stay lost.
Is this my real life?
Don't stay lost inside.
Don't stay lost.
Can you see my reflection?
I'm right here.
Will you hear my confession?
Said the fool in the mirror.
I ask myself, is this really me?
Have I become who I wanted to be?
The loss of magic day by day.
Have I lost myself along the way?
Can you see my reflection?
I'm right here.
Will you hear my confession?
Said the fool in the mirror.
Locked up inside, so many memories.
They're in the eyes, I can see.
Little child tear down that wall.
Maybe I'll save myself after all.

Don't stay lost inside.
Don't stay lost.
Can you see my reflection?
I'm right here.
Will you hear my confession?
Said the fool in the mirror.

MOMENT IN TIME

Like a watch without a hand.
Sometimes stuck in no man's land.
Part of me tries to forget.
Part of me screams no, not yet.
Like a film loop,
Playing on my mind.
Holding onto something,
Never knowing why.
Sometimes it feels to me,
Like another life.
A distant memory,
A moment in time.
Don't you ever stop and wonder,
Why you feel like crying?
It's a memory,
A moment in time.
Dreaming over, and over again.
I was so young, a child in pain.
You were standing on the other side.
I had to go, time for me to die.
Day by day, days into night.
So much time has wandered by.
Looking back is bittersweet.

Holding on to memories.
Sometimes it feels to me,
Like another life.
A distant memory,
A moment in time.
Don't you ever stop and wonder,
Why you feel like crying?
It's a memory,
A moment in time.

I Just Want to Be Me

I don't want to be the answer to your prayers.
Because that is never free.
Though I like to be the reason you are here,
I just want to be me.
Hold on,
I just need a minute.
Because it's building up inside.
And I still remember,
All the other times.
So, you think you know me.
You know, I thought I did once too.
But I'm still learning,
What I'm supposed to do.
I don't want to be the answer to your prayers.
Because that is never free.
Though I like to be the reason you are here,
I just want to be me.
Wave goodbye to that guy.
Say hello to me.
I'm not here to save you.
That's not what this should be.
I don't want to be the answer to your prayers.

Because that is never free.
Though I like to be the reason you are here,
I just want to be me.

I'm Thinking Too Fast

Hopeless chatter,
From another room.
Way out in the valley,
I can hear them still.
Wandering minds,
Plan the next move.
Up on their high horse,
On another hill.
A fine young lady,
Of Irish descent.
Burgundy hair,
And a golden glow.
Shaw once wrote,
"An Irishman's heart is nothing but his imagination."
I'm thinking too fast.
I can't keep up.
I worry about the past.
Why can't I get on with it?

HERE WE GO AGAIN

Here we go again.
I'm putting on my life vest.
I'm hoping to survive this.
So here we go again.
One more hour to kill.
The words are flying through my head.
Are you there?
Can't you feel the content of what I've said?
What you've said.
Then a thought came to me.
Once, another,
Said the very same thing.
And I was caught inside,
In a deadly slide,
A slide through time.
Here we go again.
I'm putting on my life vest.
I'm hoping to survive this.
So here we go again.

My contribution may be lost.
Too much to say,
I can't get it across.
I wish and wish all these things.
Mostly I wish life would stay out of the way.
I know it sounds stupid,
But my heart cries,
When I hear the notes.
Melody brings tears to eyes.
I wish and I wish,
I could get it across.
But life gets in the way.
Time goes by,
And melody fades.
Sometimes it hurts too much to rhyme.
I'm up late feeling what I missed.
Had something to say,
It's lost,
I'm pissed.
It's 2:00 a.m.,
And it went to waste.

SYNTHETIC WORLD

(With contributions from Mike Evans)

Something's got me restless inside.
Empty feelings and I don't know why.
Listless souls losing life in the shadows.
Wondering when they can ever let go.
Loaded words with empty meanings.
Selling someone something to believe in.
One man's right when everybody's wrong.
The thousand points of light are all gone.
I won't let synthetic world get me down.
I'm going to stand on my own.
I know I'll make it through somehow.
In humble defiance, I watch the world spin.
I'm unimpressed with what I've seen so far.
Selfish thinking replaces integrity.
When are we going to see something to believe in?
I don't see it.
Man-made troubles in a man-made world.
God sent signals to his boys and his girls.

Keep me in your heart and soul,
Save the world I have given to you.
Don't let synthetic world get you down.
You've got to stand on your own.
I know you'll make it through somehow.

HERE I AM

The words are fading.
I can't see them anymore.
And I don't remember,
What they were for.
Here I am.
Can you see me?
Here I am.
I believe in me.
You will take yourself,
Where you need to be,
And you don't need anyone else.
You don't need me.
Here I am.
Can you see me?
Here I am.
I believe in me.
I'm out of words.
I'm out of rhymes.
But I'm always looking.
Now I'm out of time.
Here I am.
Can you see me?
Here I am.

I believe in me.
Here I am.
Can you feel me?
Here I am.
I believe in me.

Just one more time,
For forever.
I don't know why,
Things can't stay the way they are.
People say,
They've got all the answers.
They'll soon find,
That it's not set up that way.
Then I look down,
To see me lying on the ground,
To keep the world,
From spinning around without me.
Holding on,
It doesn't work much anymore.
If you can find a way,
Please let me know.
There's a rainbow,
High above the highway.
It seems to me it seems to be,
A way off this crazy road.
We're all ghost towns now,
No one is there to say,
Hello, how are you?

How are you?
Chances are,
They wouldn't have liked my answer anyway.
Then I look down,
To see me lying on the ground,
To keep the world,
From spinning around without me.
Holding on,
It doesn't work much anymore.
If you can find a way,
Please let me know.
Can you hear the wind blow?
Isn't it funny how the wind survives?
Why can't you and I?

MAYBE MAKE IT RHYME

Starlight, star bright,
First star to explode tonight.
Does it feel like the world is ending soon?
Starlight, star bright,
First right move I've made tonight.
Don't you want to put it all in a tune?
Run into the wind,
And you see you're getting nowhere.
You feel you're moving backward,
Or maybe standing still.
I don't know what that means,
But I thought I would share it.
Share it with my shrink,
Maybe put it in my will.
In the middle of my day,
I feel like I am spinning,
Spinning counterclockwise.
Does it mean I'm losing time?
I don't know what that means,
But I thought I would share it.
Put it in my music,
Maybe make it rhyme.

I'm looking for acceptance,
Anywhere I can get it.
Any place that it will happen,
Anyhow and anytime.
I don't know what that means,
But I thought I would share it.
I'd never charge you for it,
That might be a crime.

PICNIC THE TREE

The trees came alive.
They walked with me all day.
We ate a picnic lunch,
On the highest green hill.
We stood in the sun.
We shuffled through the fallen leaves.
They asked me questions,
But I had no answers.
We tumbled down the mountain,
Into the water below.
We swam the river,
Until the end of the world.
We stood outside the window,
To watch life left behind.
Then we closed our eyes,
To dream again,
Of the world outside.

DAY TO DAY

Sliding slowly down hills,
Bring yourself,
Or what you will.
Swinging rusty open gates,
Paths to no one, nowhere,
You are late.
Feeding frenzied fiscal biscuits,
To the crowd,
Reality zone,
No free thinking is allowed.
Common ground,
We will pound,
Among the weak.
Broken clowns,
They run around,
To search for peace.
Money mansions,
Overlooking,
Funny farms.

Faceless patients,
Shuffle circles,
Around the yard,
Throwing stones,
And broken bones,
At no one's shadow.
Shattered dreams,
And window screams,
From below.

LITTLE BUBBLES

We went walking into the shadows,
On sentimental sidewalks.
We took a little tumble,
When we tripped upon the cracks.
We were bleeding memories,
Stuck in sediment forever.
Kept on ice for our tomorrow,
Bring party favors to the ball.
Can you open up a little longer,
To the price of little lifetimes?
Hold onto you until you're stronger,
A little broader in the heart.
Bring to the whipping post a partner,
In a silver smiling mask,
To eat the pain of your survival,
Casting shadows on the scars.
Inner city struggles,
Come to dreams in the nighttime.
Lifetime's little bubbles,
Bursting dreams into the night.
I lost your little glass slippers,
When the night was growing long.

I lost the key to my existence,
Though it was more than likely wrong.
Remember walking in the moonlight,
Breathing heavy with our fright?
Feeling sad without a reason,
I'm killing time until the ride.
We fell into the deep and dark end,
Of this giant storm,
Treading water with each other,
While we waited for the warm.
Reaching out into the thunder,
We grabbed fistfuls of discover.
Keeping notes to further science,
We were experiments in time.

LIFE AND THE LIVING

Into the line of fire,
Strolled a baby full of hopes and dreams.
Looking for peace and quiet,
But finding only brand-new screams.
Life, declared the town crier,
Is the sentence you get,
For the crime you commit.
Walking by the warning signs,
On a midnight stroll to nowhere land.
Believing in the sky,
Some would say,
Is just a waste of time.
Keeping yourself quiet,
Is the game we play,
While others run away.
Surf's up, but I'm tired,
Of all the laughter and the pain.
Lost hopes and desires.
Still, I keep a fire burning,
Through a pouring rain,
On a frozen globe in time.

Comes a warming trend,
But you are near the end.
Dark symbolic crimes,
Write the tale of who you are,
And where you've been.

TAKE THE RIDE

In the event of an emergency,
Please panic,
I always say.
It's just one of those credos to live by.
After all,
Is there a better way?
If there's anything you can depend on,
It's that you can't depend on anything.
One more phrase,
File it away.
Who knows,
You may need it someday.
When the music's over,
This is the end,
What a bleak outlook Jim had.
But who can argue with something so sad?
Walk into a wilderness,
Far away from town,
And see if you can shed,
The things you hate.
Wait there for the summer rain.
Stay through the autumn breeze,
Don't be late.

You got it,
They kept saying to me,
I really don't think I do.
But far be it from me to make a scene.
So I put myself away,
And say yes, I do.
One more piece of me,
Placed away inside a drawer.
Maybe one day,
I can spread them across the floor.
I'll pick and choose my thoughts,
And see what's there.
But for now, I'll say "Yes, sir,"
And hide away the key.
When I retire,
And may be allowed,
To say to myself,
What I didn't dare before,
I'll spend my days,
Reacquainting me with me.
I think it will be fun to see.

Until then,
Keep your eyes ahead,
And your mind asleep.
March in time,
Don't you dare miss a step.
Everyone knows,
That no one knows,
What to think themselves.
So society,
Is more than happy to help.

SILVER SAILING SHIP

In the wind,
The clouds glide by,
Throwing shadows across the sky.
In their midst,
Shines a circle,
Sailing through the waves of gray.
A silver spotlight in the mist.
A sailing sign significant.
Follow the stars,
They'll guide you home.
Silver sailing ship in a churning sea.
Through the shadows of the night,
The winter sky is crystalized,
With frozen stars.
The springtime brings the thaw.
Stars are raining from the sky.
The summer ships sailing fast,
Stronger winds are blowing.
Autumn brings the leaves and cooling breeze.
The silver ship is glowing.

RUNAWAY DREAM

(Within contributions from Dan Lesko)

Time is a synthetic measurement of
Physical existence.
Time itself does not exist.
Life itself is a runaway dream.
My mind bounces around my skull,
Leaving pieces of knowledge to drip from the walls.
So I drift away slowly in a pool of no thought,
And make a crash landing in the river of not.
Water flows downstream unless you're not there.
Some know the secret, but they'll never share.
A hill in the distance stands watch for the game.
It's been there forever; things never do change.
Break through the clouds, head straight for the sun.
No one can harm you, be careful of none.
You're coming back home now;
The trip was quite bland.
Scan the horizon for somewhere to land.
Set down near a castle where no one else goes.
The keepers are many, dressed in dark robes.
Interpreting scripture until deep in the night.
Conversing with spirits by dim candlelight.

Pictures and words from centuries long past.
Stone-cold archives, crumbling fast.
Searching for answers, have we found them at last?
Our fates depend on the spells we cast.
When the wheel stops turning the cold sweat pours.
Your body not breathing, you can't find the door.
No need to fear the nightmare,
The sweat, or the scream.
Life itself is a runaway dream.

THE ATTIC

I feel like I'm stuck in my attic.
A dusty place of used-up junk.
Thrown in a pile with the rest of the old toys.
I can wander from corner to corner,
Finding bits and pieces of myself to look at.
Each one reminds me of something lost,
Something missing.
There's a red helmet stuck in that
Apple tree on Williams Street.
It's probably gone now; it's been too many years.
There's dust and thoughts here.
And there are tears.

Once upon a time, I cared.
Now, that only makes me scared.
Circumstances, they conspire.
The only thing I feel is tired.
One line, two, hell three or four.
Who keeps count anymore?
Another pill, another whiskey.
Maybe that'll keep it all inside me.
When you push yourself so hard,
You're bound to tear yourself apart.
Not to worry, not to whine,
Soon we all run out of time.
I can't stop myself from falling.
The end just keeps on calling.
I feel like I'm going over the edge.

THEY TORE IT DOWN

I know it was a sad place.
Still, we would hang around.
The years are gone now,
The story lost.
They tore it down.
Summer night,
He was seventy-seven.
They crossed the road,
In the light of the moon.
A long hard life,
Now gone to heaven.
Silent cowards,
And their twenty-twos.
The things we recall,
Are part of the soul.
Time catches up,
Day after day.
A little bit of me,
Fades to old.
Brick by brick,
Take yesterday away.
Laughing fades,
When the story is told.

Then came the two,
We couldn't ignore.
A flight through the window,
A sign to go home.
A ghostly face looking,
Through the hole in the door.
I know it was a sad place.
Still, we would hang around.
The years are gone now,
The story lost.
They tore it down.

DISTANT THUNDER

There is a storm on the horizon.
It's looking for me.
Dark clouds, the sun is falling.
A chilling breeze.
A rumble deep in the background.
Like cannon fire.
A raven rides the rainbow,
On the other side.
It always sounds so far away.
And I was feeling safe today.
But now it's rolling closer.
Echoes over and over.
Distant thunder.
So many miles away.
It shakes my ground.
The wind screams.
Trees sway with a crying sound.
Invisible flying giants,
Blowing frozen flames.
They chase me from hide out to hide out,
Howling out my name.
And I wonder how it feels,
Up there in the thunder.

Lightning skies and oceans of wind.
Pulling you under.
Soaring far away.
The raven gives chase.
Diving through the rainbow,
Into a sunny summer day.

GYPSY SAFARI UNDERGROUND

For days and days,
They did appear.
A mob of whispered shadows in my ear.
The greatest cause of all would bring them down.
The gypsy safari underground.
You wonder why,
You wander around,
When your heart tells your brain,
Settle down.
Winding down steps quickly,
From shadows beneath me.
Ships go down,
Tied to fence posts in the sea.
Whistle Dixie,
While your charcoal cross crumbles.
Offer up,
Dissolution and plunder.
Alternate routes laid,
With blood were paid.
Brave the cold,
To bow and bend your way.
Melting worlds collide in tides.
With currents giving chase.

Then with a rumble,
I tumble,
To the edge.
To force the fools,
To face the dead.

THE GAME

When one game is over,
Another begins.
Empty stare,
Empty words fill the air.
Why don't you catch the five o'clock train to you?
And take a tour of what used to be there.
The sun comes up,
You pull the shades down.
Turning over and over,
Avoiding the ground.
Welcome back,
I wish I could say.
Turning over and over,
You keep rolling away.
You don't want to have to deal with you.
Based on nothing,
To blame is best.
Paint your shield,
A smiling face.
Live in your attic,
And forget all the rest.
Somewhere, sometime,
You'll have to come out.

Late at night,
You're lurking about.
Fear and lonely,
Are the emotions today.
Always wondering why,
You turned me away.
I'm sick and deathly tired of the game.
Don't tell me your secrets.
Don't tell me your name.
I just want someone who is safe to forget.

SOMETHING TO SEE

On nights with no moon,
The stars take the stage.
Through silver clouds,
They fight their way.
On a pitch-black curtain,
They play.
It was like that,
The first time I saw her.
Diamond eyes,
Cut through the cold night air.
Her hair flew around her face,
Dancing in the wind,
Like a wild thing without a care.
She imprisoned my heart and lonely soul.
I had no strength to fight.
I felt her hot and cold fingers around my heart.
I watched myself disappear into the night.
Be careful what you wish for,
Were her first words to me.
Funny, I thought, I hadn't felt her read my mind.

Down the side of the hill,
I watched pieces of me fall away.
No matter how I tried,
I could not stop my flight.

With a crying sound,
You came winding down,
Back into the past.
I wonder what you are,
How you fell so far,
Down into the dark.
Keep me staring hard,
At an empty jar,
We used to call our hearts.
Dusty on a shelf,
A mirage of self,
The outside full of scars.
I feel,
I am,
Less than what you are looking for.
When will you return?
The memory burns,
From deep within my mind.

I'll come home someday,
I heard the memory say,
But it's not in time.
I feel,
I am,
Less than what you are looking for.

DESERT STORM

Just try to smile a while.
Count the raindrops one by one.
Watch the storm come over the mountains,
And take away the desert sun.
Dark clouds roll off the horizon,
Onto a sandy plain.
Howling wind through the hills.
Dryness bathed in rain.
Close your eyes.
Let yourself go,
To a quiet place.
Listen to the thunder.
Feel the wind on your aching face.
Feel the lightning light you while
Your mind wanders.
Flashing and rumbling, the storm cleans the land.
Rivers of rain washing the sin.
The sun appears, drying the sand.
It hangs around until the storm comes again.

She walked away.
Why I'll never know.
But that's for her to suffer.
I have my own suffering to do.
When I think back now,
I can't recall the day.
I do know how I felt.
But I can't feel that now.
Memories replace the pain.
Must be my own way of coping.
Over the years those will also fade,
And once again I'll be left with nothing.
Wait a moment,
I think again,
Now I recall,
It rained that day.
And when she was gone,
The sun arrived.
Now I recall,
I sat and smiled.

FEELING EASY

(For Grandpa Crowley, with
contributions from Chris Kaercher)

You are the spirit,
Which carries me through life.
Words and music merge together.
If there comes a time,
When things just aren't right,
It comes together there is harmony.
Sometimes the melody is haunting.
It makes you feel the memory.
I think it's time,
To feel what must be felt.
If the music helps you,
Then let it out.
Let the music ease your mind.
Release your soul tonight.
Give yourself a chance to find,
Feeling easy feels so right.
I used to hide,
Hide my heart and soul,
Deny myself the memory.

I let it out,
And now I'm free.
Somebody's singing inside of me.
Let the music ease your mind.
Release your soul tonight.
Give yourself a chance to find,
Feeling easy feels so right.

Walk in the Summer Sun

Long ago I was a child,
I had a love I'd never met.
Recurring dreams would bring her face,
And when I woke, an emptiness.
The dream seemed so real.
I could feel her there beside me.
Our hearts were trapped in different times.
With passing days, worlds fade away.
I was much too young to feel that warm glow.
I was much too young to feel so alone.
I was much too young.
We used to walk in the summer sun.
From time to time, I still remember.
Along with her face comes the pain.
And there's already too much in this world.
Where should I go to escape?
I was much too young to fight the tears.
I was much too young to feel the fear.
I was much too young.
We used to walk in the summer sun.

1 />

I COULDN'T SAY WHY

During a sleepy silken Egyptian dream,
I found myself holding sweet smells of melody,
Making a deal with ancient green mummies,
Watching you writing hieroglyphics on the wall.
You were so far down into the sand that day,
I had to start a dig just to see your face.
And when I hit the bottom level, it was desert sky.
I had to welcome you home, but I couldn't say why.
In your reflection, I see broken fairy tales.
Look down, I'm bleeding puddles in the sand.
They rise like dragons breathing
Flames of midnight blue,
Exposing inside to a cold and distant hand.
Immaculate pools of dead and dying dreams,
Drain into the desert, seeping below the Sphinx.
They lie there waiting to drown a drowning man,
Innocently slipping into this dreamland.
You were so far down into the sand that day,
I had to start a dig just to see your face.
And when I hit the bottom level, it was desert sky.
I had to welcome you home, but I couldn't say why.

THE DREAM PLACE

In my mind,
While I sleep,
I see visions.
I can see visions of peace.
Rolling hills,
With a view of life.
A perfect perspective makes everything right.
All is lush and pure and clear.
A peaceful playground of thought.
To feel what's right and what is not.
Oh, in my mind,
I find answers to life.
The dream place makes everything right.
It makes everything right.
Feelings are warm and true and bright.
An honesty of the heart and mind.
Through time we will weep.
But we can see visions.
We can see visions of peace.
A seemingly soothing sanctuary for the soul.
Mending mental misconceptions makes me whole.
And time, it will keep.
The visions are of me.

That's important, don't you see?
Oh, in my mind,
I find answers to life.
The dream place makes everything right.
It makes everything right.

I Think It Was Nashville

We took off down the road,
Driving all night long.
You were running to chase your dream.
I was running from something inside of me.
You wanted to be a star.
I just wanted to sing my songs.
I think it was Nashville.
I remember the rain.
I think it was Nashville.
Fell in love that day.
As I recall it was 2 a.m.,
When you kissed me.
After years on the road,
I can tell you're done.
You're tired it's been too long.
I guess I'll go on alone.
You wanted to go back home.
I still needed to sing my songs.
I think it was Nashville.
I remember the rain.
I think it was Nashville.
Fell in love that day.

As I recall it was 2 a.m.,
When you walked away.
Some dive bar in your town, I was playing,
When you came around.
I was wishing the years away.
You were wishing I could stay.
You said, come back home to me.
I said, I'm where I need to be.
I think it was Nashville.
I remember the rain.
I think it was Nashville.
Fell in love that day.
As I recall it was 2 a.m.,
When you walked away.
I think it was Nashville.

We've been here before.
Hey, you say, I can fix this.
Then you see it in my eyes.
Not this time.
This is where you cry.
For us, there's no tomorrow.
I thought I'd spend my life with you.
This is where we cry.
If time could just stand still,
Maybe then I could have saved us.
But there's nothing left inside.
Say goodbye.
This is where you cry.
For us, there's no tomorrow.
I thought I'd spend my life with you.
This is where we cry.
We've been here before.
Hey, you say, I can fix this.
Then you see it in my eyes.
Say goodbye.
This is where you cry.
For us there's no tomorrow.
I thought I'd spend my life with you.

AUTUMN RENAISSANCE

There's a harvest moon up in the sky tonight.
I'm mesmerized by the orange light.
And if you reach up high,
You can hold the stars,
As the clouds roll by,
Racing for tomorrow.
Sunburnt leaves,
Rustle across the ground.
Clear cool wind,
Is blowing all around.
I am alive, fills my mind.
Western dusk,
Is calling softly for the sun.
Look around you.
Do you feel alive,
In this autumn full of life?
Look around you.
Do you feel you'll survive,
Another autumn renaissance?
Dark ponds sparkling.
Coincidental depth.
Existence reappears,
With every single breath.

Deep greens,
Turning golden in the breeze.
Burning skies,
Are full of spirits flying free.
Look around you.
Do you feel alive,
In this autumn full of life?
Look around you.
Do you feel you'll survive,
Another autumn renaissance?

FROZEN IN TIME

Do you remember me?
Standing in the corner.
Avoiding the cool kids.
Blending in with the background.
Our hearts were on the run.
We talked until we saw the sun.
I recall you said goodbye,
And I wondered, should I even try.
A hill on the edge of town.
You walked away,
The moment gone.
I tried to run.
You tried to hide.
Your face and my hopes,
Frozen in time.

JUST IN CASE

Just in case you don't remember,
This is what it used to feel like.
This is where we used to dream.
Hiding for a long time.
Inside and in between.
Looking for something,
Deep within your eyes,
Under brilliant starry skies.
Dark exciting nights.
Holding on to you and me.
Trying not to think of what will be.

IF YOU REALLY WANT TO

(With contributions from Dan Lesko)

I wake up in the morning,
Feeling déjà vu.
I've got to be somewhere,
Doing something for you.
But I don't even feel good.
I don't feel right,
I don't feel real.
I see you on the street now,
Hello, how are you?
You're doing okay,
Don't give a shit what the doctors say.
But I don't even feel good.
I don't feel right,
I don't feel real.
My head begins spinning,
And I just don't know how I feel.
You can use me,
If you really want to.
You can use me,
Because I know you really want to.
Yes, you do.

I've got to catch my breath now,
So my heart doesn't explode.
You see I'm getting dizzy,
I'm off my feet, and I'm off the road.
But I don't even feel good.
I don't feel right,
I don't feel real.
My heart has been breaking,
And I'm just not sure how I feel.
You can use me,
If you really want to.
You can use me,
Because I know you really want to.

WHERE DO WE GO FROM HERE?

I saw a picture just the other day,
Some old lady walking barefoot in the street.
Those without are shuffling their lives away,
While those who have are dragging their feet.
I heard a man just the other day,
He was talking a real fine speech.
Telling us how everything's okay,
Everything's okay.
Politicians are dragging their feet.
It makes me wonder what's in store for us.
Where do we go from here?
Where do we go from here?
I saw my lady just the other day.
She said, you know, I don't know you anymore.
I looked around and saw that time had slipped away.
She said goodbye, and then she closed the door.
Do you recall the eyes of the ones we trusted,
With our lives and our feelings?
Do you recall?
It makes me wonder what's in store for us.
Where do we go from here?
Where do we go from here?

I Can't Stay

(With contributions from Dan Lesko)

It took me thirty-seven tries,
Until I could say goodbye.
I'm done playing little games.
You won't miss me anyway.
I can't stay here.
I need some peace of mind.
There's too much pain here.
I'm leaving it all behind.
I can't stay here,
Because you're there and you're
There and you're there.
I can't stay here.
I just want to disappear.
I think I'm over you.
At least I hope so.
Sunshine only knows my smile.
Pain fades with every mile.
I can't stay here.
I need some peace of mind.
There's too much pain here.
I'm leaving it all behind.

I can't stay here,
Because you're there and you're
There and you're there.
I can't stay here.
I just want to disappear.
Taking pills to stay happy.
I got the best they had.
When you wash them down with whiskey.
It feels like you're floating free.
I just want the tunes to keep playing.
That's all I'm really saying.
It's going to make everything alright.
I'll be heading for the better times.
Now we're heading for better times.

THE NEXT BEST THING

(With contributions from Dan Lesko)

Let me know,
When you find what you are looking for.
You think it's easy,
But you don't know what you're in for.
I'll see you sometime with a look,
A look on your face.
I told you before,
I told you in the first place.
You're happy having fun you're alright.
You've got nowhere else to go tonight.
You're looking for someone with a big diamond ring.
I'm not the one but I'm the next best thing.
And when you're willing,
Are you certain that you're able,
To take a chance,
Like they do in the fables?
Will you live happily ever after,
Or fall in disgrace?
Don't believe the bullshit,
I told you in the first place.
You're happy having fun you're alright.

141

You've got nowhere else to go tonight.
You're looking for someone with a big diamond ring.
It's not me, but I'm the next best thing.
Pretty quickly,
The hours turn to years.
The end is coming,
You can see it from here.
Like a blast from the past,
I suddenly see your face.
I never should have loved you,
I told me in the first place.
You're happy having fun you're alright.
You've got nowhere else to go tonight.
You're looking for someone with a big diamond ring.
It's not me, but I'm the next best thing.

In a windswept rain,
I can see your face,
Fading fast but not yet gone.
You run from the past,
It moves you along.
27 miles to Akron.
I'm hoping that you're there when I get home.
27 miles to Akron.
I fear I've been away far too long.
You chased me through golden rows of grass,
Catching me whole but standing too close.
Miles away, the gold grass froze.
I tried in so many ways,
To forget the tears that day.
In time yours will fade,
But mine will never go away.
Now I'm down on my knees,
And tears fill my eyes.
I pray to a God,
I never believed in,
When I open my eyes,
It's you I am seeing.

27 miles to Akron.
I'm hoping that you're there when I get home.
27 miles to Akron.
I fear I've been away far too long.

HOSTILE WATERS

(With contributions from Bill Evans)

Crying in the waves.
The North Atlantic graveyard.
Wavering nature,
Unbalanced by man.
The sea is red with sorrow.
The beach inhales the gloom.
Will there be any left tomorrow?
Will we be finished soon?
And who decides who will live,
And who is going to die?
Bastards taking casualties,
Can someone tell me why?
Tell me why.
Wooden ships powered by hatred.
White sails filled with greed.
Didn't we know they're sacred?
Like man is supposed to be.
And who decides who will live,
And who is going to die?

Bastards taking casualties,
Can someone tell me why?
Tell me why.
Does anybody cry?

I'll Be Waiting

Just this morning,
The sun came over the hill.
And every morning,
You know that it will.
Some days,
The gloom hangs around.
And you can surely feel it,
All over town.
When this world has got you down,
You want to smile,
But you've only got a frown.
Just remember,
The sun comes back around.
When I see you walking up my lane,
It makes no difference that the sun never came.
Because your love warms me like the rays of the sun.
So come on clouds,
You can hang around with me.
When this world has got you down,
You want to smile,
But you've only got a frown.
Just remember,
The sun comes back around.

That star has fallen for the day.
And I can see you walking away.
I'll be waiting for another day.
I'll be waiting for you to stay.
When this world has got you down,
You want to smile,
But you've only got a frown.
Just remember,
The sun comes back around.

SPHERICAL WONDERLAND

You wake up,
You look down,
Reality is nowhere around.
There were crystal cities,
With little red bubbles of sun.
And my head was spinning.
My head was spinning around.
And I swear I'm floating,
Nowhere near the ground.
I'm flying through my dreams,
And everything I see,
Is crystal clear.
I'm in a spherical wonderland.
My mind takes me by the hand.
Through the sun and into the city.
I found the entrance.
The door.
The door is inside of your mind.
And my head was spinning.
My head was spinning around.
And I swear I'm floating,
Nowhere near the ground.

I'm flying through my dreams,
And everything I see,
Is crystal clear.
I'm in a spherical wonderland.
My mind takes me by the hand.
Through the sun and into the city.
I found the entrance.
The door.
The door is inside of your mind.
Look inside.

WHY NOT FOREVER?

(With Chris Kaercher)

How can it be,
You can bring the sunshine to my life?
How can I make you see,
Just how much you mean to me?
We can be happy,
For a while.
And I would be happy,
Just to see your smile.
When I'm holding you,
The world around me fades away.
If I could only stay,
In your arms forever.
We can be happy,
For a while.
And I would be happy,
Just to see your smile.
The years they shall pass,
Our two lives, they will go on.
Will the feelings last?
I can't forget I love you always.

EARLY MORNING RAINBOW

In the morning light,
Colors tumble from the sky.
Separate hues dance through the haze,
To blaze a trail for the day.
Shades of gray survive the rise,
Lingering lazily about the sky.
Longing for clouds to shadow their foes,
Awaiting dusk, they're the rainbow's ghost.
Early morning rainbow,
Spray my day with light.
Early morning rainbow,
Stealing color from the night.
And when I see your smile,
I can't imagine a cloudy day.
An endless time of sunshine.
Why must the day go by?
Early morning rainbow,
Spray my day with light.
Early morning rainbow,
Stealing color from the night.

Every day is a gift of time,
Time for you and I.
When your smile begins to fade,
We'll sail the rainbow away.

RIDE AMONG THE MEADOWS

(With contributions by Bill Evans)

Tears,
Falling from the sky.
Breeze,
Wash them from my eyes.
Noble beast, take me away.
Save me from another day.
Climb aboard,
Ride the wind.
Distant shores,
Waving through the meadows.
Sail away,
Leaving worry far behind.
Climb aboard,
Ride among the meadows.
Fear,
Holding me so tight.
Breeze,
Wash them from my mind.
Noble beast, take me away.
Save me from another day.

Climb aboard,
Ride the wind.
Distant shores,
Waving through the meadows.
Sail away,
Leaving worry far behind.
Climb aboard,
Ride among the meadows.

MORNING DEW

(With contributions from Bill Evans)

In the still of the first light of dawn,
Come fly through the trees.
I see the crystal cities floating there.
Here comes the sun,
Yes, it's finally rising,
They shine, they shine.
Like a sign from the one,
Who allows us to be here.
And so I partake,
Of the cool spring water.
Birds flying, birds flying, birds flying high,
In the blue sky.
It sits in the trees,
And it clings to the leaves,
And it smiles at you and me.
Drip, drip, dripping away,
In a labyrinth of streams.
We are naive,
When it comes to the things that we see.

There is a reason for morning dew,
And me and you.
Just because the sun chases dew from the leaves,
Doesn't mean it won't be here tomorrow.
It is a sign of second chances.

JOURNEY OF A FEELING

(With Mike Evans)

Captains sail along,
In a September song.
Vessels venture through,
Leaking and listing.
Ghostly mist,
Stinging desperate faces.
Dreams into memories.
Lasting scars.
The journey of a feeling,
It's like sailing an empty sea.
The journey of a feeling,
Will take you places you've never seen.
Seek the elusive heart.
Emotional sails.
Recall the endless journey,
To believe in the love.
Heaven's nautical nature,
Will vindicate the strong ones,
While taking its toll
Among the weak and shallow.

AURORA

Constellations,
In the Northern Hemisphere.
Falling rain,
That shines into the night.
Bring me the stars Orion,
On your northern flight.
Then someone turned on the northern lights,
Streaking lightning through the sky,
To turn on the goddess in distant lands,
Like neon-green crystals inside sand.
You spent your lifetime chasing daughters,
Seven of them in all.
But your soul was in Aurora,
The Goddess of the Dawn.
Was it the myth or was it magic?
Was it the story written at the end of time?
Did you believe you'd capture the journey,
In a bottle of blood-red wine?
Wasn't your sanity in jeopardy,
In your unachievable dream?
Didn't you see the light in front of you,
Or did the brightness blind your eyes?

POCKET FULL OF MEMORIES

I watched my shadow on the sidewalk,
I tried not to overthink what it meant and my place.
Having reached that day, the old age of six,
I let the thought linger, then went about my play.
I remember sitting in the apple tree on Sundays,
Reading books from the library;
To other worlds I escaped.
The breeze in the trees around me,
I'm gone for a while.
A warm memory that I keep
In my pocket still, for a smile.
Watching the stars,
Smelling the autumn leaves,
Counting Monte Carlo cars,
Hearing faint bells of trucks with ice cream.
Riding bikes until my legs ache,
Taking me to the other side of the world each day.
Trading baseball cards,
A rookie Bench, what would you pay?
Flashlight tag and ghost in the graveyard,
The Big Red Machine riding the nighttime air,
Echoes of laughter, I hear them now,
Summer nights; a timeless time shared.

You were looking for a place to hide.
I was looking for my peace of mind.
Another chance to save someone.
Not me, not again, I'm done.
This time, you're on your own.
It's time for me to stand alone.
Another one of my stupid mistakes,
Another soul I tried to save.
Maybe this will make me worth something.
Growing up I was torn down.
My self-esteem always under siege.
Too short, freckled face, skinny legs.
Laugh upon laugh upon laugh, so hard to breathe.
No matter what I was able to accomplish,
It was never enough.
My sense of self-worth became a
straggler I dragged along behind.
Year over year, fifty-nine gone by,
Somehow, I have survived.
I wish it hadn't taken so long to learn,
The open wounds cauterized by
Years of burn on top of burn.
Expect to stand alone,

but surround yourself with the worthy,
Not those who tear others down,
So that they may lift themselves up.
Surround yourself with the worthy.
True friends who laugh and find joy in life,
Those who value and respect.
Do that, and you never stand alone.

ONE DAY SOON

All around, nothing but the deepest dark,
But one day soon, the sun.
No way out of my head, nowhere to go,
But one day soon, the sun.
Thunder of worst fears, filling the ears.
Winds of unknown gust, biting and stinging.
Rumble of oncoming suffer, building fears.
Hopes in ruins, shiver and cringing.
Mind paralyzed and bending,
I can't recall how to breathe.
A nightmare never ending,
A feeding frenzy, senses leave.
All around, nothing but the deepest dark,
But one day soon, the sun.
No way out of my head, nowhere to go,
But one day soon, the sun.
The dawn will come.
Darkness fades, if you stand against it.

About the Author

Jason Crowley is a storyteller, a musician, and an artist. Graduating with honors in 1992 from the Central Ohio Technical College in the field of computer science, Jason had a successful career in the technology field for over thirty years. A right-brained guy stuck in a left-brained world, Jason managed to carve out time for his creative passions: creating music, writing, and painting.